A CHILD'S BOOK OF

Flowers

A CHILD'S BOOK OF
Flowers

Janet Marsh

HUTCHINSON
London Sydney Auckland Johannesburg

For George

First published in 1993

1 3 5 7 9 10 8 6 4 2

Janet Marsh has asserted her right under
the Copyright, Designs and Patents Act, 1988
to be identified as the author and illustrator of this work

First published in the United Kingdom in 1993 by
Hutchinson Children's Books
Random House UK Limited
20 Vauxhall Bridge Road, London SW1V 2SA

Random House Australia (Pty) Limited
20 Alfred Street, Milsons Point, Sydney,
New South Wales 2061, Australia

Random House New Zealand Limited
18 Poland Road, Glenfield
Auckland 10, New Zealand

Random House South Africa (Pty) Limited
PO Box 337, Bergvlei 2012, South Africa

Random House UK Limited Reg. No. 954009

A CIP catalogue record for this book
is available from the British Library

Designed by Rowan Seymour
ISBN 0 09 176231 6
Printed in Hong Kong

The publishers gratefully acknowledge Frederick Warne and Co. for
permission to reproduce 'The Song of the Snowdrop Fairy' by
Cicely Mary Barker, © The Estate of Cicely Mary Barker, 1923, 1926,
1940, 1944, 1948, 1990, and 'The Song of the Pansy Fairy' by Cicely
Mary Barker, © The Estate of Cicely Mary Barker, 1934, 1990; and
Methuen Children's Books for permission to reproduce 'Daffodowndilly' and an extract from 'The Dormouse and the Doctor',
both from *When We Were Very Young* by A.A. Milne.

Contents

A Note on Flowers

On a summer's day, a buzzing bee is attracted to a brightly-coloured flower
and lands on its petals. The bee is looking for nectar and, as it searches, it
brushes tiny grains of pollen from the male part of the flower (the stamen) on
to the female part (the pistil). Some time after the pollen has reached the pistil
a new seed begins to grow. And when the flower has died all that remains is
its fruit with the seed inside. Finally the seed may be blown by the wind on
to the earth, where it will begin to grow into a new plant.

The parts of a flower

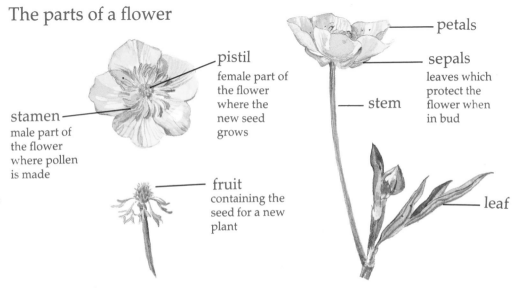

pistil
female part of
the flower
where the
new seed
grows

stamen
male part of
the flower
where pollen
is made

fruit
containing the
seed for a new
plant

petals

sepals
leaves which
protect the
flower when
in bud

stem

leaf

How long does a flowering plant live?

The plants in this book all belong to one of the following groups:

Annuals grow from seed, flower and die all in one year.
Biennials grow stems and leaves in the first year, flower in the second year
and then die.
Perennials live for at least three years. Some, such as lupins, die down during
the winter and grow up again in the spring. Others, for example roses,
simply stop growing leaves and flowering during the winter.
Bulbs can last many years. Each new season a stem grows up through the
earth from the bulb. After flowering the plant dies down.

Snowdrop

At the end of a long winter, there is no prettier sight than a clump of snowdrops bravely flowering beneath the branches of a leafless tree. The delicate drooping flowers are made up of three white petals, which hide three smaller petals tinged with green. By late February the blue-grey leaves are almost the same height as the flowers, which are now in full bloom. The flowers have a strong, sweet smell.

Annual

COLOUR   white
HEIGHT   20cms
FLOWERING   January – March
LOCATION   woods, gardens,
        by rivers and streams

The snowdrop's name probably came from the German, *Schneetropfen*. Before this the snowdrop was known as the early white violet. Another less appealing name for it was death's flower. In several countries it was thought unlucky to bring snowdrops into the house.

from ST AGNES' EVE

Make thou my spirit pure and clear
As are the frosty skies,
Or the first snowdrop of the year
That in my bosom lies.

Alfred Lord Tennyson

THE SONG OF THE SNOWDROP FAIRY

Deep sleeps the Winter, cold, wet and grey;
Surely all the world is dead; Spring is far away.
Wait! the world shall waken; it is not dead, for lo,
The Fair Maids of February stand in the snow!

Cicely Mary Barker

Long ago, the snowdrop was called 'the fair maid of February'. In English villages young maidens would gather snowdrops and wear them at the festival of Candlemas in February, as a sign of purity.

Crocus

Bulb

COLOUR   white, yellow, mauve, purple, striped

HEIGHT   5cms

FLOWERING   January – April, September – December

Crocus is the Latin name for saffron, the cooking ingredient, which is found in the flower of a variety of crocus known as the saffron crocus.

The crocus is one of the earliest flowers to appear in spring. After a long winter, its bright colours cheer up the garden. At first, its flowers look rather funnel-shaped; but when they are in full bloom, they open out until they look more like deep cups. Crocuses are often planted under trees or on lawns in great numbers so that in spring they look like beautiful living carpets.

The purple crocus has been seen as a royal flower – the regal crocus in purple and gold. The poet Longfellow imagined a yellow crocus in Christ's crown:

Hail to the King of Bethlehem
Who weareth in his diadem
The yellow crocus for the gem
Of his authority!

CROCUSES
The sunrise tints the dew
The yellow crocuses are out
And I must pick a few.

                    Anon

Over six hundred years ago, a pilgrim smuggled some saffron crocus bulbs into the town of Walden in Essex. Once planted, the bulbs flourished and the town soon became known as Saffron Walden.

Violet

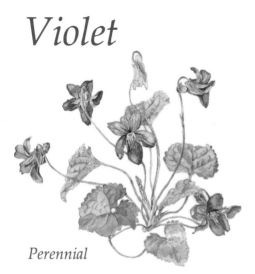

Of all the violets, only the sweet violet is scented. It has been a popular choice in gardens for hundreds of years. The Ancient Greeks made purple dye from sweet violets, and the Arabs used them to make a drink called sherbet. Its flowers are still dried to make perfume or sweet-smelling pot pourri. Sugared violets make a delicious sweet.

Perennial

COLOUR   violet, blue, pink and white
HEIGHT   5-15cms
FLOWERING   February – June
LOCATION   woods, hedgerows, gardens

The violet is meant to have been created by Zeus, king of the gods. The name violet comes from the Latin word for the flower, *Viola*.

from LUCY
A violet by a mossy stone
Half hidden from the eye!
Fair as a star, when only one
Is shining in the sky.
　　　　　　William Wordsworth

from THE FAIREST FLOWER
The violet in her greenwood bower,
Where birchen boughs and hazels mingle,
May boast herself the fairest flower,
In glen, or copse, or forest dingle.
　　　　　　Sir Walter Scott

from THROUGH THE LOOKING GLASS
'I never saw anybody that looked
stupider,' a Violet said, so suddenly, that
Alice quite jumped; for it hadn't spoken
before.
　　'Hold your tongue!' cried the Tiger-lily.
'As if you ever saw anybody! You keep
your head under the leaves, and snore
away there till you know no more what's
going on in the world, than if you were a
bud!'

　　　　　　Lewis Carroll

Queen Victoria was very fond of violets. This made them so popular that soon men were wearing buttonholes of violets to work every morning. They probably bought them from street-sellers who would call:

Violets sir! Buy my violets!
Sweet violets sir!
All a-growing!

17

Primrose

Perennial

COLOUR   yellow
HEIGHT   10cms
FLOWERING   March – May
LOCATION   Woods, hedgerows,
          gardens

When primroses are in flower, you know that spring is here at last! The primrose's name comes from the Latin, *prima rosa*, meaning first rose. In Devon the primrose is also known as butter rose, after the creamy farmhouse butter which is made there.

The primrose's flowers are a soft pale yellow. They grow on hairy pink stalks, surrounded by soft wrinkled leaves. If you lift up the leaves, you can see thick veins underneath. Primroses are low-growing plants and are easily hidden. But even in the dappled shade of a wood, you may be lucky enough to spot one glowing like a nugget of pale gold. Primroses have always had a special place in folklore. In the Middle Ages country people used to put them on cowshed floors on May Day, to keep witches away from cattle. Primroses were also used to make love potions.

CRYSTALLISED PRIMROSES

To make pretty crystallised primroses you will need:
1 small bunch fresh primroses from your garden
½ tsp gum tragacanth (buy from your chemist)
2 tbsp triple strength rose-water
caster sugar
scissors
small screw-top jar
wire tray
small paintbrush
airtight tin

Pour the gum tragacanth and rose-water into the screw-top jar and leave in a warm place for 24 hours, shaking the jar from time to time. Then cut the primrose stems to 3 cms and, holding the first flower by its stem, paint both sides of each petal with the gum and water mixture. Sprinkle lightly with caster sugar.

When you have done this with all the flowers, put them on a wire tray to dry overnight. Next day, snip off the stems and store the crystallised flowers in an airtight tin. Use them to decorate special cakes. They look wonderful on a chocolate birthday cake!

Daffodil

Bulb

COLOUR   yellow, white
HEIGHT   16cms (wild),
         32cms (garden)
FLOWERING   March – May
LOCATION   Open woods, damp
           grassland, gardens

The flower we usually call daffodil also shares the name *Narcissus* with a famous character form legend. Narcissus fell in love with his own beautiful reflection in a pool. He pined away, broken-hearted and was transformed into a lovely flower.

In Wales the daffodil is a national emblem and is worn on the first day of March, Saint David's Day, in honour of their patron saint. In England, where it's sometimes called daffydowndilly, the daffodil has been popular for over four hundred years. There are many different kinds of daffodil, although all have a 'trumpet' at their centre surrounded by six petals. They range in colour from white to deepest yellow, and some are tinged with orange. Daffodils grow from bulbs which are planted in the autumn.

DAFFODOWNDILLY

She wore her yellow sun-bonnet
She wore her greenest gown;
She turned to the south wind
And curtsied up and down.
She turned to the sunlight
And shook her yellow head,
And whispered to her neighbour:
'Winter is dead.'

A. A. Milne

from DAFFODILS

I wander'd lonely as a cloud
That floats on high oe'r vales and hills,
When all at once I saw a crowd,
A host of golden daffodils;
Beside the lake, beneath the trees,
Fluttering and dancing in the breeze.

William Wordsworth

It used to be the custom for children to give daffodils to their mothers on Easter Day, saying:

Daffodillies yellow,
Daffodillies gay,
To put upon the table
On Easter Day.

21

Daisy

Perennial

COLOUR   white with a yellow
              centre
HEIGHT   5-8cms
FLOWERING   early spring to late
                summer
LOCATION   lawns and meadows

The name daisy means day's eye.
It is a good name for a flower
which opens during the day to
show its yellow centre (its eye) and
closes at sunset.

The pretty white daisy is the
commonest of our wild flowers. You
can find it growing in short grass on
lawns, and also in long meadow grass.
The daisy flower has lots of narrow
oval petals which may be tipped with
pink. The centre of the flower is bright
yellow. The daisy's spoon-shaped
leaves grow flat against the ground,
where they are protected from grazing
animals and lawnmowers.

Little girls pull the petals off a daisy, one at a time, to find out if *he loves me* (first petal) or *he loves me not* (second petal). Of course they hope that the last petal they pluck will show that *he loves me*.

Here is another chart for pulling petals off:

One I love, two I love,
Three I love, I say,
Four I love with all my heart,
Five I cast away;
Six he loves, seven she loves,
Eight both love,
Nine he comes, ten he tarries,
Eleven he courts, twelve he marries.

HOW TO MAKE A DAISY CHAIN

Pick some daisies with long stalks. Take one daisy and split its stalk with your thumbnail near the end. Thread a second stem through the split and then make a split in this stem. Thread a third stem through the second split – and so on. Finally join the two ends of the chain together to make a necklace or crown.

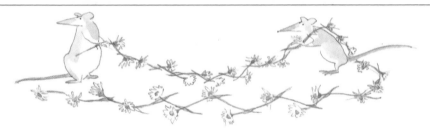

Dandelion

Perennial

COLOUR   yellow
HEIGHT   15-30cms
FLOWERING   March – October
LOCATION   gardens, meadows,
            wasteland

The name dandelion comes from the French words, *dent de lion*, meaning lion's tooth. The dandelion was called this because its petals look like the golden teeth of a royal lion.

There are hundreds of different kinds of dandelion. You can see them almost all year round, although they grow especially well in April and May. The dandelion plant has long leaves with jagged edges and yellow flowers. Each flower is made up of lots of tiny flowers, all joined to a main stalk. When the dandelion has flowered, the petals dry up and seeds begin to grow. A few days later, a fluffy dandelion 'clock' appears. When a light wind blows, the ripe seeds float away like miniature parachutes.

The dandelion 'clock' has up to one hundred and eighty seeds. If you blow on the 'clock' once and every seed comes off, it should be one o'clock. If you need two puffs to blow them all away, it should be two o'clock – and so on.

THE DANDELION

What's o'clock, what's o'clock?
Count and see.
One o'clock, two o'clock,
One, two and three.
Three o'clock, four o'clock,
Five o'clock, tea?

RIDDLE

First you see me in the grass
Dressed in yellow gay;
Next I am in dainty white,
Then I fly away.

Dandelions have many uses in the kitchen. Young dandelion leaves taste good in salads; coffee can be made from the plant's long root, and its flowers can be used to make wine.

Tulip

Bulb

COLOUR   nearly all
HEIGHT   19-47cms
FLOWERING   April – May
LOCATION   gardens

The tulip first grew on the banks of the river Bosphorus in Turkey. It came to Europe in the sixteenth century and was soon the most prized of flowers. In Holland huge prices were paid for a single bulb. Even today the Dutch are famous for their tulips. The first tulips were usually bright scarlet, with a black spot at the bottom of each petal. Now they come in almost any colour, shape and size. Lots of tulips planted together make a dazzling bed of colour in any spring garden. Some stand tall and upright; others fold back their petals and lean towards the sun.

The name tulip comes from the Persian word *tulipant*, meaning turban. Compare the shape of a tulip flower with a turban and you will see why.

26

I've got a pretty tulip
In my little flower-bed.
If you would like I'll give it you –
It's yellow striped with red.

Kate Greenaway

Persian legend tells the sad story of a young man who threw himself from a cliff when he found out his beloved had died. Where his blood was spilt, a mass of red tulips grew up and so the flower became the symbol of perfect love. Yellow tulips stand for hopeless love and purple tulips for a love which will never die.

from A FAR PLACE
White groups and pink, red, crimson, and lemon-yellow,
And the yellow-and-red-streaked tulips once loved by a boy;
Red and yellow their stiff and varnished petals,
And the scent of them stings me still with a youthful joy.

J.C. Squire

27

Bluebell

The bluebell is a member of the lily family. It has long narrow green leaves and a spray of blue bell-shaped flowers. The mouth of each bell curls back, so that it looks rather like a tiny blue bonnet – one of the many country names the bluebell has been given. Years ago people used to scrape the root of the bluebell for the slime which coated it. They used the slime for glue. Nowadays the bluebell is protected and should not be picked.

Bulb

COLOUR   blue, white, pink
HEIGHT   5-15cms
FLOWERING   April – May
LOCATION   woods

Hundreds of years ago the bluebell, or wild hyacinth, was known as *Hyacinthus angelica*. According to Greek legend, when the god Apollo accidentally killed his best friend Hyacinth, he was so sad he decided to turn him into the beautiful flower we now call bluebell.

IN AND OUT THE DUSTY BLUEBELLS is a traditional dancing game for ten or more children. This is how it is played. First the children choose a leader, who stands aside. Then the other children stand in a circle and, raising their arms, join hands to make lots of arches. The leader skips through the arches as the children sing:

In and out the dusty bluebells
In and out the dusty bluebells
In and out the dusty bluebells
Who will be my master?

When they have finished, the leader stands behind another child and taps her on the shoulder, singing:

Tippy-tippy tap-toe on my shoulder,
Tippy-tippy tap-toe on my shoulder,
Tippy-tippy tap-toe on my shoulder,
You will be my master.

This child then becomes the new leader. The old leader stands behind her and they both weave in and out of the children in the circle. And so the game continues until the circle is broken and the children fall on the floor in a heap.

Cowslip

Perennial

COLOUR   yellow
HEIGHT   15-23cms
FLOWERING   April – June
LOCATION   gardens, meadows,
woodland

The meaning of the cowslip's pretty name is – cow dung! The cowslip was probably given this name because it grows well in fields where cattle graze. Its Latin name, *Primula veris*, is much nicer. This means first of spring.

The once common cowslip now grows wild only in lonely meadows and woodland, and along some motorways. Luckily, more and more people are growing cowslips in their gardens. The cowslip's rich yellow flowers hang in clusters at the top of long velvety stalks. Each flower is made up of five petals joined together to form a long tube. The cowslip's pale green wrinkled leaves grow in tufts near the ground.

from THE TEMPEST
Where the bee sucks, there suck I
In a cowslip's bell I lie;
There I couch when owls do cry.

                    Shakespeare

THE COWSLIP
Then came the cowslip, like a dancer at the fair,
She spread her little mat of green and on it danced she,
With a fillet round her happy brow,
A golden fillet round her brow,
And rubies in her hair.

                    Sidney Dobell

LOVE AND AGE
I play'd with you 'mid cowslip blowing,
When I was six and you were four,
When garlands weaving, flower balls throwing
Were pleasures soon to please no more.
Through groves and meads o'er grass and heather,
With little playmates, to and fro,
We wander'd hand in hand together;
But that was sixty years ago.

                    Thomas Love Peacock

COWSLIP BALLS
Cowslip balls are made by picking off clusters of flowers and hanging them over a piece of string. Gently ease the flowers together before pulling the string up into a knot.

The result is a pretty ball of flowers held neatly in place by the hidden string.

Carnation and Pink

Most carnations are grown in greenhouses because they dislike cold and wet. When cut, they are often used in flower arrangements. The carnation's near relative, the pink, is less fussy and will grow outdoors. Carnation flowers have five feathered petals at the top of long stems. They come in many different colours and have a spicy smell similar to cloves. Carnations are popular buttonholes on special occasions, particularly weddings.

Annual and Biennial

COLOUR   nearly all
HEIGHT   30-100cms
FLOWERING   May – August
LOCATION   gardens

The name carnation comes from the word coronation. Carnations were often used in wreaths and garlands to crown the 'queen' of a festival. They are sometimes also called gillyflowers.

Though carnations and pinks look very alike, if you compare them you will see that carnations have bigger flowers, broader leaves and longer stems than pinks. Pinks don't get their name because of their colour, but from the frilly edges of their petals, which look as if they have been notched or pinked.

In Devon it used to be the custom to make a present of scented gloves at Easter.

The rose is red, the violets blue,
The gillyflower sweet, and so are you;
These are the words you bade me say
For a pair of new gloves on Easter day.

There are two wild pinks in this country. One is the maiden pink (so called because it is the colour of a young girl's blushing cheek), and the cheddar pink. The cheddar pink is found only on the limestone cliffs of the Cheddar Gorge in Somerset, and is protected by law. There are many kinds of pink which grow in the garden.

from PINKS
The pinks along my garden walks
have all shot forth their summer stalks,
Thronging their buds 'mong tulips hot,
And blue forget-me-not.

Robert Bridges

Snapdragon

The snapdragon is a favourite flower not only of gardeners, but also of children. To find out why, place your forefinger and thumb either side of a snapdragon's mouth and gently squeeze. See how wide you can make your snapdragon's mouth open. The snapdragon's flowers grow on firm, straight spikes and are coloured anything from white, cream and yellow to pink, scarlet and crimson.

Annual

COLOUR   white, yellow, pink, red
          (garden); also pink,
          purple, yellow (wild)
HEIGHT   10-90cms
FLOWERING   May – September
LOCATION   gardens; dry, bare
            places, rocks,
            walls (wild)

You can tell how the snapdragon got its name when you look at the flower, which is rather like a mouth. When a bee lands on the lower lip of the 'mouth', the flower opens and the bee enters to collect the nectar. When the bee flies away, the snapdragon's 'mouth' snaps shut.

In some parts of England children
call snapdragons bunny rabbit
flowers because their shape is like
the mouth of a rabbit.

People used to believe that snapdragons had special powers to
destroy spells. They thought a garland of snapdragons could
keep you safe from witches and perhaps even dragons.

Forget-me-not

Biennial

COLOUR   blue
HEIGHT   15-20cms
FLOWERING   May – September
LOCATION   damp, shady places

Forget-me-nots often grow thickly together. The curled buds grow in rows shaped like a scorpion's tail, and forget-me-nots were once called scorpion grass. The flowers turn from pink to pale blue as they open and have a yellow eye at their centre. Their leaves are pale green.

The forget-me-not gets its name from the romantic story of a knight who went out to pick flowers for his lady and was drowned. As the water swept him away, he threw the flowers to his beloved, crying 'Forget me not!' and so they were named.

Then the blossoms blue to the bank he threw
Ere he sank in the eddying tide:
And 'Lady, I'm gone, thine own knight true,
Forget me not,' he cried.

The farewell pledge the lady caught,
And hence, as legends say,
The flower is a sign to awaken thought
Of friends who are far away.

Anon

PRESSING FLOWERS

It is very simple to press flowers even if you do not have a flower press. Soon after picking them, arrange the flowers you have chosen on a sheet of blotting paper. Cover them with another sheet and place between the pages of an old telephone directory. Put one or two heavy books on the directory and leave for at least a month. Many pretty gifts can be made from pressed flowers. To make a flower bookmark take a piece of white card (4cm x 20cm). Glue some pressed flowers on one side of the card and cover both sides with clear self-adhesive plastic film. Using different sizes of card you can also make flower pictures and greeting cards.

Honeysuckle

Perennial

COLOUR   creamy yellow
HEIGHT   300-600cms
FLOWERING   May, June,
             September
LOCATION   woods, hedges,
             gardens

Country children used to pick
honeysuckle to suck the honey
from its flowers – and this pastime
gave the plant its name.

The honeysuckle is a twining, climbing plant which scrambles up hedges and trees and over garden walls and trellises. Shakespeare called it by the older name of caprifole, or goat leaf because, like the goat, it can climb to places normally out of reach. Shakespeare also called it by its other popular name, woodbine, because it can bind itself around young trees so tightly they cannot grow. The honeysuckle's stem is tough, always twining from left to right. Its yellow flowers, tinged with red, are long and narrow and clustered together in delicate sprays. Because of the flowers' shape, honeysuckle is called lady's fingers in some places.

During the summer the flowers have a deliciously sweet scent which wafts through the air. People used to build honeysuckle bowers where they could sit in the shade and enjoy the perfume. After the flowers have bloomed, clusters of dark red berries appear, which are highly poisonous.

Buttercup

Perennial

COLOUR   yellow
HEIGHT   15-60cms
FLOWERING   May – October
LOCATION   gardens, meadows,
            wasteland

The buttercup's correct name is crowfoot. Look at the shape of its jagged leaves and you will see why. Each leaf is separated into three parts, with the middle part stretching beyond the other two. So the whole leaf looks like the mark of a bird's foot. The buttercup flower is a bright shiny yellow. It usually has five cup-shaped petals.

The buttercup was given its name because people once thought that its yellow flowers increased the amount of butter in cows' milk. In fact cows dislike the taste of buttercups and leave them well alone. Even so it is a favourite name for a cow.

Hold a buttercup under a friend's chin to find out if they like butter. If you can see a deep yellow shadow on his or her skin, it means your friend likes butter very much. But remember that because younger children have fairer skins than older children or adults, you will probably find that it is your younger friends who appear to like butter the most.

THE BUTTERCUP

Do I like butter? You want to know
Whether I do like butter or no.
A buttercup under my chin will show
Whether I do like butter or no.

BUTTERCUPS AND DAISIES

Buttercups and daisies,
Oh, the pretty flowers;
Coming ere the Springtime,
To tell of sunny hours.

Mary Howitt

She made him a feast at his earnest wish
Of eggs and buttercups fried with fish.

Edward Lear

Geranium

The geranium family includes over a hundred different types of plant which grow throughout the world. In Britain there are sixteen kinds of wild geranium. All have flowers with five flattish petals which blossom in groups. One of the commonest is a plant called Herb Robert, or Poor Robin. This is a delicate-looking, hairy plant, with spreading stalks and small flowers of a rich crimson colour. Its leaves have a very strong, nasty smell and so in some areas it used to be called 'Stinking Bob'.

Perennial

COLOUR   white, pink, red, purple
HEIGHT   to 30cms (wild);
         to 40cms (garden)
FLOWERING   May – September
LOCATION   meadows, hedgerows
         (wild); gardens

One of the most common types of geranium is the wild geranium, or cranesbill. The cranesbill was called this because the seed pod of its flower is shaped like the bill of a bird known as a crane.

The meadow cranesbill, which grows by the roadside, has violet-coloured flowers, with red veins on each petal. These veins guide bees to the nectar in the centre of the flower.

For many of us the most familiar geraniums are the plants with brightly coloured heads of flowers and large leaves, which fill gardens and windowboxes every summer. In fact these are really pelargoniums – cousins of geraniums – and grow wild in South Africa.

from THE DORMOUSE AND THE DOCTOR
There once was a dormouse who lived in a bed
of delphiniums (blue) and geraniums (red)
And all the day long he'd a wonderful view
of geraniums (red) and delphiniums (blue).

A.A. Milne

When you give someone a geranium it is a sign of true friendship.

Pansy

The pansy is a dainty, low-growing flower. Its five velvety petals are so soft that if you stroke one against your cheek you can scarcely feel it. The petals may be one colour or a combination of two or more. The pansy has had many different names over the centuries, many of which have something to do with love: kiss-and-look-up, love-a-li-do, love-in-idleness.

Biennial

COLOUR white, yellow, blue, mauve, violet, purple
HEIGHT 9cms
FLOWERING May – September
LOCATION gardens, fields, wasteland

The name pansy comes from the French word *pensee*, which means thought. The wild pansy is also known as heartsease. It may have been called this because the pansy's two side petals look as if they are kissing, and the kiss gives ease of heart – or heartsease.

PANSY

Pansy and petunia
Periwinkle, pink –
How to choose the best of them,
Leaving out the rest of them
That is hard I think.

Poppy with its pepper-pots,
Polyanthus, pea –
Though I won't slight the rest,
Isn't pansy quite the best
Quite the best for P?

Black and brown and velvety
Purple, yellow, red;
Loved by people big and small,
All who plant and dig at all
In a garden bed.

Cicely Mary Barker

In Shakespeare's *A Midsummer Night's Dream*, the fairy king, Oberon, quarrels with his queen, Titania. As a punishment, he commands a servant to squeeze the juice of love-in-idleness into sleeping Titania's eyes, which will make her fall in love with the first thing she sees when she wakes. This turns out to be Bottom, a man with the head of a donkey!

Lupin

Lupins are tall, soldier-like plants with long spikes of flowers often a metre tall. If grown at the back of a flower bed, they look as if they are guarding the plants in front. There are four main kinds of lupin, which all belong to the pea family. The garden lupin is the tallest of the four. It has lots of flower spikes, which may be any colour from white through to orange, red and indigo. The wild lupin is shorter, and is always blue or purple. The tree lupin looks like a bush and has shorter spikes of yellow, white or mauve.

Perennial

COLOUR blue, purple (wild); also pink, white and yellow (garden)
HEIGHT to 60cms (wild); to 100cms (garden)
FLOWERING June – August
LOCATION rivers, shingle, moors (wild); gardens

The name lupin comes from the Latin *lupus*, a wolf. It may have been given this name because people once believed that the lupin's deep roots harmed the soil. The lupin was the wicked wolf of the flower world!

Foxglove

Biennial

COLOUR   pink, purple, yellow or
         white
HEIGHT   60-150cms
FLOWERING   May – September
LOCATION   woods, heathland,
         hillsides, gardens

The name foxglove may have
come from the nickname folk's
gloves, (folks meaning fairies).
Another explanation is that
naughty fairies gave foxgloves to
some equally naughty foxes who
used the flowers to soften the
sound of their paws as they crept
up to the hen house.

The foxglove grows almost anywhere.
It is a very tall plant with large oval
leaves growing up a long stem. At the
top of the stem, there are lots of
brightly coloured flowers. These
slightly drooping, trumpet-like flowers
are usually pink outside, and speckled
within. In Wales foxgloves are called
elves' gloves, in Scotland bloody
fingers and in Ireland fairy thimbles.

Foxglove flowers may look like perfect
hats or gloves for children's fingers,
but remember they are poisonous!

Poppy

One of the most beautiful sights of summer must be a cornfield full of red poppies. Eight different kinds of poppy commonly grow in Britain. The Welsh poppy, the horned poppy and the Arctic poppy are yellow. The opium poppy is lilac, pink or white, while the long-headed, rough, prickly and common poppies are bright red.

Annual

COLOUR   scarlet, pink, lilac,
          yellow, white
HEIGHT   30-80cms
FLOWERING   June – September
LOCATION   wasteland, roadsides,
          gardens

The common poppy is the one you see on roadsides and wasteland, it is a tall shaggy plant with crumpled scarlet flowers. At the centre of each flower are its seeds, held in little capsules until ready to be released.

Poppy seeds left in the ground start to grow if the ground is disturbed. During the first world war, poppies sprang up everywhyere. Today we remember the dead by buying paper poppies each November, the month the war ended.

from IN FLANDERS FIELDS
In Flanders fields the poppies blow
Between the crosses, row on row
That mark our place, and in the sky
The larks, still bravely singing, fly
Scarce heard amid the guns below.
                    John McCrae

Poppies cannot be picked – they wilt immediately:

from TAM O'SHANTER
But pleasures are like poppies spread –
You seize the flow'r, its bloom is shed.
                    Robert Burns

Children used to be afraid of picking poppies because they thought a thunderstorm would follow. They called poppies Thunderbolts, Thundercups, Thunder-flowers or Lightnings.

Hollyhock

Biennial

COLOUR white, pale yellow, pink,
        deep red
HEIGHT 150-200cms
FLOWERING June – September
LOCATION gardens

The hollyhock was once also called hockleaf, because many people believed that its leaves cured horses with swollen hocks (a part of the leg). People also thought (wrongly) that hockleaf came from the Holy Land. In time, hockleaf and Holy land became simply hollyhock.

In fact, the hollyhock is a Chinese plant which was brought to Europe over four hundred years ago. The Chinese particularly admired it for its strength. This is not surprising when you find out that hollyhocks are the tallest flowers in the garden, and their sturdy stems reach a height of over two metres! Hollyhock flowers are large and crinkled, measuring between ten and fifteen centimetres across. The colours of the flowers range from white and yellow to scarlet, crimson and purple. Beneath the flower spike grow huge soft rounded leaves.

from A FAR PLACE
The broad-leaved tapering many-shielded hollyhocks
Stood like pillars and shone to the August sun

J.C. Squire

from THE CHOICE
When skies are blue and days are bright,
A kitchen garden's my delight,
Set round with rows of decent box,
And blowsy girls of hollyhocks.

Katherine Tynan Hinkson

from THE FLOWERS
All the names I know from nurse;
Gardener's garters, Shepherd's purse,
Batchelor's buttons, Lady's smock,
And the Lady Hollyhock.

Robert Louis Stevenson

Lavender

Perennial

Lavender grows in a bush. It has silvery-green leaves and rings of flowers at the top of a slender stem. There are more than thirty kinds of lavender, which produce flowers in several different colours. For hundreds of years people have used dried lavender flowers to scent linen and to perfume rooms. Lavender petals were once used to make sweet-smelling icing for cakes, while lavender oil was supposed to help you digest your food. Today lavender is still an important ingredient of perfume and scented soap.

COLOUR   lilac, purple, pink or white
HEIGHT   39-90cms
FLOWERING   June – September
LOCATION   gardens

Lavender gets its name from the Latin word to wash, *lavare*. The Romans, who spoke Latin, used lavender when doing their laundry.

LAVENDER'S BLUE

Lavender's blue, dilly, dilly,
Lavender's green;
When I am King, dilly, dilly,
You shall be Queen.
Call up your men, dilly, dilly,
Set them to work,
Some to the plough, dilly, dilly,
Some to the cart.
Some to make hay, dilly, dilly,
Some to cut corn,
While you and I, dilly, dilly,
Keep ourselves warm.

LAVENDER BAGS

Pick the lavender when it is still in bud, and hang it up to dry. Then strip the buds off the stems and gather them into small bags. Sew up the bags and place between sheets, towels and clothes. The scent should last until the lavender is next in bud.

Sweet pea

The sweet pea has silky two-petalled flowers which grow in groups on slender stems. They come in a wide variety of colours. If the flowers are picked regularly, more and more blossom throughout the summer. They have a strong sweet scent. The sweet pea plant grows upwards on delicate tendrils, which wind around any support they can find. People often grow sweet peas up a garden fence or a frame of garden canes.

Annual

COLOUR   various
HEIGHT   2-3m
FLOWERING   June – September
LOCATION   gardens

The sweet pea originally came from the island of Sicily. Its Latin name, *Lathyrus odoratus*, hints at its strong scent. Can you guess why?

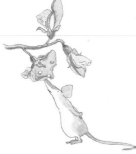

from A COTTAGE GARDEN
And on the crowded spot that pales enclose
The white and scarlet daisy rears in rows,
Training the trailing peas in clusters neat,
Perfuming evening with a luscious sweet –
                                    John Clare

SWEET PEA
There are sweet peas, on tip toe for a flight
With wings of gentle flush o'er delicate white
And taper fingers catching at all things
To bind them all about with tiny rings.
                                    John Keats

Rose

There are probably more kinds of rose than any other flower. New varieties are produced each year and are often named after famous people or important events. The roses we grow in gardens as bushes, shrubs or climbers have thorny stems, flowers of many petals and often a wonderful fragrance. Wild roses have smaller and simpler flowers and can be shrubs or climbers. Jam and syrup is made from the roses' seed pods which are known as hips. The rose is an English national emblem, and is worn on 23rd April, to celebrate St George's Day.

Perennial

COLOUR   all shades of pink, orange, yellow, red and white
HEIGHT   19-200cms
FLOWERING   June – September
LOCATION   gardens, hedgerows

According to legend the queen of flowers was created by the Greek gods and goddesses from a spirit of nature called a nymph. They gave it the wonderful scent, brightness, charm and joy the rose still has today.

The Ancient Egyptians put rose petals in their food and wine and filled their mattresses and pillows with rose leaves. Today we still use sweet-smelling dried petals in pot pourri and oil of roses in perfume.

from TO THE VIRGINS, TO MAKE MUCH OF TIME
Gather ye Rose-buds while ye may,
Old time is still a flying:
And this same flower that smiles to day,
To morrow will be dying.

                                        Robert Herrick

R was once a little rose
  Rosy
  Posy
  Nosy
  Rosy
Blows-y-grows-y
Little Rose!

          Edward Lear

O my Luve's like a red red rose
That's newly sprung in June:
O my Luve's like the melodie
That's sweetly play'd in tune.

                        Robert Burns

TO MAKE A PAPER ROSE

Take a long strip of tissue paper (12cm x 75cm) and fold in two without flattening the folded edge. Then fold one top corner over to make a diagonal edge and start rolling up the strip from here, pinching and squeezing the

bottom as you go. Before you finish rolling, fold over the other top corner. Push a piece of wire into the base of the flower and secure with sticky tape.

Thistle

Perennial

COLOUR   purple, blue, yellow, white

HEIGHT   30-150cms

FLOWERING   July – October

LOCATION   hedgerows, wasteland

The family name for thistle comes from the Greek word, *echinos*, which means hedgehog. Who could think of a better name for a plant with such rounded spiky flowers?

There are several different kinds of thistle, ranging from the low-growing stemless thistle to the scented musk thistle and the giant spear thistle. The stout, spiny stems and prickly leaves guard a soft, cottony flower. The seeds inside the flower have feathery hairs called thistledown. Thistledown is known for its silkiness. The thistle is Scotland's national flower. It was chosen for its prickliness and its beautiful colours at a time when the Scots were often at war.

People used to eat the leaves and stalks of thistles such as the milk thistle. They removed the prickles, then boiled the leaves and peeled the stalks to make winter salad and a rhubarb-like pudding. The soft down from the stem and leaves of the cotton thistle was collected for stuffing pillows, cushions and beds.

Cut thistles in May, they grow in a day.
Cut them in June, that is too soon.
Cut them in July, then they die.

When thistles are deeply in love
Don't their bristles make cuddles too rough?
It must be so prickly –
No! For thistles it's tickly,
And one kiss is never enough.

Anon

My Flower Notes